**Margaret Thatcher's
History of the World**

Margaret Thatcher's
History of
the World

Compiled by Andrew Moncur
Illustrated by David Austin

The **Guardian/Fourth Estate** • **London**

First published in Great Britain by
Fourth Estate Limited
Classic House
113 Westbourne Grove
London W2 4PU

British Library Cataloguing in Publication Data is available
ISBN 1-872180-80-9

Printed & bound in Great Britain by Richard Clay Ltd,
Bungay, Suffolk

Contents

	Introduction	1
1	In the beginning	7
2	Ancient times	17
3	The Dark Ages	27
4	1067 and all that	35
5	Merrie England	49
6	Enterprise Initiatives	63
7	Undesirable elements	73
8	Our gallant lads	83
9	Victorian values	89
10	The Age of Enlightenment	105
	List of contributors	119

Introduction

ON JANUARY 30, 1649, King Charles I walked on to a balcony in Whitehall and his head fell off. The very British death of a monarch. So unlike the deplorable events in Paris 140 years later, when the French were more than usually revolting.

Mrs Margaret Thatcher, Prime Minister and diplomatist, has, of course, strong views about the teaching of history (stirring and British, naturally) and about the true significance of events in the recorded past of other nations. During her visit to Paris for the climax of celebrations marking the bicentenary of the French Revolution, she was asked by an interviewer whether the upheaval of 1789 held any universal message.

"No, pardon me for saying, but I think not," she replied. But, didn't France create the Rights of Man?

"Certainly not . . ." said Mrs Thatcher, recalling our own (very British) Magna Carta of 1215. The French were left with little room for misunderstanding. The significance of their Revolution? Roughly nil. Well, so much for France's contribution to global affairs. That's set them straight.

This exercise in putting the world's past to rights prompted the Guardian diary column to challenge readers: why not compile the Margaret Thatcher World History Book?

Here is the outcome, covering — from a very special viewpoint — major events from the dawn of time up to the Age of Enlightenment (the period of the present administration, that is to say). This volume is the work of Guardian readers, whose contributions to the better understanding of world history are warmly acknowledged.

Andrew Moncur

I

In the beginning

And on the eighth day **God** had to attend a Restart interview.

God's creation of the world: an example of the worst kind of restrictive practices; just think what might have been achieved with seven-day working and no closed shop.

I fail to see what possible objections Arthur Scargill can have when even the most cursory reading of Genesis will show that six-day working has the blessing of God Himself.

When God said "Let there be light" he meant, of course, subject to the market economy.

Original sin: Adam and Eve made themselves deliberately homeless.

The Flood: wasteful deployment of resources in public sector services.

The Flood: note that God awarded the

ark contract to a small family firm; an
early form of Enterprise Scheme.

Sodom and Gomorrah: cities with left-
controlled councils which encouraged
so-called "rights" for deviant minorities.
The resultant breakdown of moral
standards polluted the environment so
severely that it necessitated a drastic
public cleansing programme costing
millions.

On the sad fate of Lot's wife: as I have
said repeatedly, there is nothing
whatsoever to be gained by looking back.

Jesus of Nazareth: definitely not one
of us.

Jesus: I know we never actually met but I'm sure he wouldn't mind me using his first name.

Mary and Joseph demonstrated a positive appreciation of the duties involved in meeting the Community Charge.

King Herod: inventor of a novel method of birth control which would have been completely successful were it not for the incompetence of his advisers and some small presentational problems.

As for the flight of the holy family into Egypt: frit.

Moneylenders in the temple: showed the pressing need for a stock exchange in Jerusalem.

No-one would have remembered the **Good Samaritan** if he'd only had good intentions. He had money as well.

Forsaking one's father and mother and deliberately making oneself homeless to follow an intinerant troublemaker are not compatible with the Christian values for which this country stands.

Of course, water quality has been a worry for a very long time — one has to wonder what He was walking on.

Jesus: a vagrant who paid the rightful penalty for attempting to introduce politics into Christianity.

Judas: a contemporary of Jesus who understood the benefits of a free market economy.

II

Ancient times

Since about **6,000 BC** Europe has been separated from Britain.

The Pyramids: a marvellous example of what can be achieved with non-union labour and the correct managerial approach.

Socrates: a typical teacher who forced peace studies on his pupils, encouraged subversion, promoted homosexuality and undermined the family. A clear illustration of the need for a national curriculum.

Every **Spartan** had been trained from birth to acquire a full portfolio in Sparta plc. This enabled him to fight fearlessly, fearlessly and wholeheartedly, knowing that his dependants could participate in generous take-over bids and not to have to rely on any nanny state for handouts.

The 300 Spartans' valiant resistance to the Persian host (480 BC): a classic case of restrictive practices leading to overmanning.

Diogenes: no moaning Minnie; unable to find a cardboard box, he lived in a barrel, with no benefits whatsoever.

Archimedes: the first person to benefit from the privatisation of water

We are simply extending Archimedean principles by screwing the public to raise water profits.

Romulus and Remus: the true originators of care in the community; in the spirit of free enterprise they went out and found their own wolf rather than expecting one to be provided by the state.

Spartacus was eventually crucified for persistently refusing to price himself into a job.

Boadicea: a one-woman campaign incorporating a privatised transport system.

The reason that Boadicea's rebellion did not succeed is that the handbag had not then been invented.

Boadicea's rebellion; an early example of a strong woman leader fighting the imposition of European socialism on Britain — roads, sewers, bathhouses, all provided by the state

Boadicea: now it can be told. It wasn't suicide. The water was poisoned.

Then **Hadrian** hit on a wonderful idea for dealing with the Scots.

Hadrian's Wall is a relic of foreign incompetence, having been built 100 miles too far up accurately to mark the north-south divide.

The folly of the Scots in building Hadrian's Wall was that much-needed revenues of tourism were denied them despite kindly advice from English authorities on the subject.

410 AD, the **Sacking of Rome:** protest by the ordinary ratepayer against overspending by the Greater Rome Council on grandiose buildings, libraries, grants for circus owners and other minority groups.

Fall of the Roman Empire: the Visigoths were very *heterosexual*.

III

The Dark Ages

The Dark Ages: that unfortunate period before our scientists discovered the benefits of cheap, clean, nuclear electricity

What caused the break-up of **King Arthur's** Round Table? All those beer and sandwich meetings, that's what.

Attila the Hun (406-453) not only

successfully privatised under-used Roman assets, he cut the swollen imperial bureaucracy down to size.

Of course, we've had these brain drains from England before. As you will remember, **King Offa** built a great dyke to prevent . . .

King Alfred (849-99) at least ensured that no salmonella would be found in the cakes.

Had energy been privatised in the 9th Century Alfred would have had to think twice before being feckless enough to burn the cakes.

King Alfred assured the housewife that the cakes were safe in his hands.

Those burnt cakes could have been avoided if Alfred's wife had been in her proper place — the home — instead of work-sharing with her leftist feminist friend.

In 878, or thereabouts, Alfred the Great passed a law defining compensation for accidental death by a falling tree. The subsequent influx of Danes is the first recorded example of immigrants coming to England to take advantage or our advanced social security provisions.

The **Vikings** were demonstrating the dangers of letting hooligans travel abroad without proper ID cards.

Danegeld was an early form of personal health insurance.

Unfortunately, **Canute** failed to package his message to the waves.

You know, if only Canute had stood firm he would have got the tide to turn eventually.

Vlad the Impaler disliked equivocation and felt compelled to pin people down.

IV

1067 and all that . . .

The Norman Conquest: Surely another Conservative election victory in Chingford.

The **Battle of Hastings** showed how careless people were about their eyes before charges for NHS eye tests were introduced.

1066: the usual appalling advice from the Foreign Office lost Harold the battle of Hastings and submitted the nation to centuries of dangerous French influence

1066: Wasn't really important.

William the Conqueror's harrying of the North: the happy consequence of a *successful* political strategy to root out the enemy within.

The **Bayeux tapestry** was an early experiment in identifying supporters for an away match.

St Francis of Assisi (1181-1226): one of the earliest Christians who interfered

in politics. He deceived with his prayers,
seemingly innocuous and even
superficially attractive but capable of
being of being thrown cruelly back into
the face of anyone who subsequently
tried to use them.

Genghis Khan: a fine example of an
enterprising young man who got on his
horse.

The Mongol Empire: Genghis was one of
us. A Khan-do person.

Of course, Genghis Khan was the other
great statesperson to realise that there
was no alternative.

Thomas à Beckett: a perfect example of what should happen to a planted official who goes native.

Thomas à Beckett: a mid-term reshuffle was needed to bring new blood into the cabinet.

Henry II said that Archbishop Beckett had his full support.

Richard I and Blondel: An excellent demonstration of the lack of a need for government intervention in the location of hostages.

Robin Hood: a terrorist.

Robin Hood failed to found a viable free-
enterprise school of archery, instead
wasting his time on those too spoon-fed
to help themselves.

The depradations of Robin Hood and his
gang were only made possible by a
distorted adoption of green policies.

The **sale of indulgences:** a welcome
introduction of market forces in a
monolithic and inefficient bureaucracy.

Edward I (1239-1307): his castle-
building programme created much-
needed jobs in the Welsh building
industry.

Robert the Bruce and William Wallace: narrow-minded Scots who didn't appreciate the advantages of sharing oil wealth.

Robert the Bruce learned from watching the spider that spiders and nations in partnership — like Scotland and England — prosper if the the larger (female) partner devours the smaller.

Edward II (1284-1327): an early example of Clause 28 in action.

The **Black Death** (1348) was an insidious socialist plot to raise the wages of labour and thus add an extra twist to inflation.

The Black Death was an innovative
scheme designed to ease both the
development pressures in the South-East
of England and unemplyment nationwide.

The career of the **Black Prince**
demonstrates that in this country it has
always been possible for those of ability
to get on, regardless of colour.

English **settlement of Ireland:** An early
example of the concern for green issues
and devotion to land which has always
distinguished the Tory party.

It was unthinkable that democratic
Britain should witness barbarism such as
was seen in France — so we held our
Terror in Ireland.

The **Wars of the Roses:** an unseemly
quarrel between York and Lancaster for
the right to host a Garden Festival that
would bring much-needed employment
to their deprived inner cities.

Rough Justice was inevitable. Keeping
children in the Tower was not suitable
grounds for exemption from the Poll Tax.

Joan of Arc (1412-1431) posed a direct
threat to the task force.

Joan of Arc: what did women's lib ever do
for her?

France ensured her place in history
when she helped the English, in 1415, to

just that confidence and heightened morale needed for their own role on the world stage - and incidentally, gave Shakespeare his finest film script.

1492: **Christopher Columbus** set out to sail to India but accidentally found his way to America. Such a feat of incompetent navigation is utterly typical of the unreliability of ships.

On April 22, 1518, **Hernando Cortes** and his gallant task force arrived at Vera Cruz, far away on the other side of the Atlantic, on the first stage of their mission to liberate the local Aztec population from the burden of an oppressive and reactionary government.

Lucrezia Borgia: a prominent Italian
stateswoman with an utterly efficient
approach to disposing of fractious
politicians.

V

Merrie England

The **Peasants' Revolt:** Yes, don't they.

The peasants did *not* revolt. There was simply a rush of people eager to pay their poll tax.

What tiler?

At least **Henry VIII** made sure his wives didn't become a burden on the state.

Pilgrimage of Grace: my gracious visits to every disaster in the land.

John Knox: for pity's sake, someone let him in.

In 1562 **Sir John Hawkins,** the free market trader, was taking the under-privileged to the West Indies for a game of cricket.

Richard III offered his kingdom for a horse which shows, in real terms, how much better we are doing in the battle against inflation.

Mary Queen of Scots: a moaning minnie from the north.

The 100 Years War: a conflict that prevented the Channel Islands falling to foreign domination. Rejoice!

The **dissolution of the monasteries** ended centuries of outmoded and restrictive medieval practices, released the stranglehold of the Roman Catholic monopoly on worship and the closed shop of ecclesiastical preferment, restored land for productive use by the business sector and brought stagnating capital into the exchequer.

We had been shockingly treaty-ed by Rome so we had to stand up and fight our corner. Demanding our money back, we privatised the Church's assets, thus laying the foundations of modern civilisation.

Dissolution of the monasteries: a radical British government demonstrated to the Roman Catholic Church the benefits of privatisation.

Another reason why Henry VIII had to sack the monasteries was because they wouldn't accept that God is British.

Henry VIII: the greatest exponent of freedom of choice. You could choose either to agree with him or to have your head chopped off.

The **Elizabethan era:** when state enemies were seen off by a woman with an axe.

Queen Elizabeth I owed everything to her devoted Cecil.

The defeat of the **Armada** by a privatised Navy under Sir Francis Drake was only the first example of our ability to cause individual warships of the enemy fleet to sail in opposite directions at the same time.

In 1588, after a disastrous summer season, the Spaniards decided to drop out of the cruise market.

Execution of **Charles I,** 1649: never happened.

Charles I's difficulties were simply due to a failure in presentation.

On January 30, 1649, Charles I stepped from a window of the Whitehall Banqueting Hall and his head fell off. His son was abroad at the time and, travel being a little difficult in those days, he did not return to England for 11 years and therefore was not crowned Charles II until 1660.

Small civil war. Only one monarch killed.

And you know, Charles repeatedly said

that the **Nell Gwynne** association was always intended to demonstrate the advantages of putting state catering and ancillary services out to private tender.

Judge Jeffreys originated the short, sharp shock treatment for juvenile delinquents which proved extremely successful in reducing the number of repeating offenders.

Judge Jeffreys: a great penal reformer. He was determined that prisons should not be overcrowded.

1666: Emergency services were unable to respond effectively to the **Great Fire** due to dreadful mismanagement by extremist Whig-controlled Greater London Council.

Samuel Pepys, civil servant and diarist.An unfortunate combination, which should have been stopped for the good of the nation and generations as yet unborn.

We call the **1688 Revolution** bloodless because the bloody parts happened in Ireland and Scotland which, of course, don't count.

The **Massacre of Glencoe** (1692) was ordered by the then authorities to explain to the Macdonalds the error of their ways in not registering for the Community Charge.

While seeking to evade Mr Campbell, the Community Charge officer for that bit at the top of Yorkshire, the Macdonalds were tragically trapped in a severe snowstorm at Glencoe and perished before our splendid rescue services could reach them. We were, of course, unable to visit them in hospital.

Robert the Bruce: a misguided and ungrateful Scotsman whose spider-fixation utterly prevented him from appreciating the benefits of rule from Westminster.

The **Renaissance** started in Grantham and spread throughout Europe, as far as the Italian hamlets of Florence and Rome.

We British have a long tradition of generous toleration of minority groups.

After all, in **William and Mary** we had the world's first transvestite monarch.

The Enlightenment: the means by which voters are led to understand that a large balance of payments deficit is the sign of a successful, Conservative-managed economy.

VI

Enterprise Initiatives

A fine and compassionate example of our early enterprise culture was undoubtedly **Sir John Hawkyns'** self-financing scheme to provide free transport to an area of expanding job opportunities for underprivileged ethnic minorities.

The **slave trade** ended an acute unemployment crisis in West Africa.

Moreover, the slave auctions gave these people an idea of their true value to society.

The British welfare state began centuries ago when we gave millions of underprivileged Africans free Caribbean holidays.

The slave trade: a splendid example of British initiative in developing the package tour.

Slave trade: an excellent example of private enterprise training the workers without jobs to do the jobs without workers.

There were those who struggled to end the Spanish government's monopoly of Peruvian gold. Privateers, using their own venture capital, worked to secure wider ownership of this resource.

Galileo failed to understand that, while pure research is of course of immense interest, the primary aim of scientists must be to foster useful applications of their knowledge, so that they can make their contribution to the creation of the nation's wealth.

The **South Sea Bubble** (1710): the second most impressive British economic miracle.

1720: the Chancellor describes the collapse of the South Sea Company as a temporary blip.

1776: the loss-making British colonies in **North America** were privatised and sold off to the highest bidder, a local consortium headed by a Mr G. Washington.

The **Black Hole:** if Calcutta had had the poll tax it could have really cleaned up.

The Black Hole: the tragic outcome of some high-spirited Britishers playing the childish game of sardines.

Highland Clearances: you must

remember that we gave thousands the opportunity to take their enterprise and money-management skills abroad and, what's more, attracted foreign investment into land improvement in Scotland.

Baby farming was an example of admirable private initiative as against the nanny welfare state.

The **Poor Law** was so called because it was so woefully inadequate in making the undeserving stand on their own two feet.

Botany Bay: the Club Med of the 18th century.

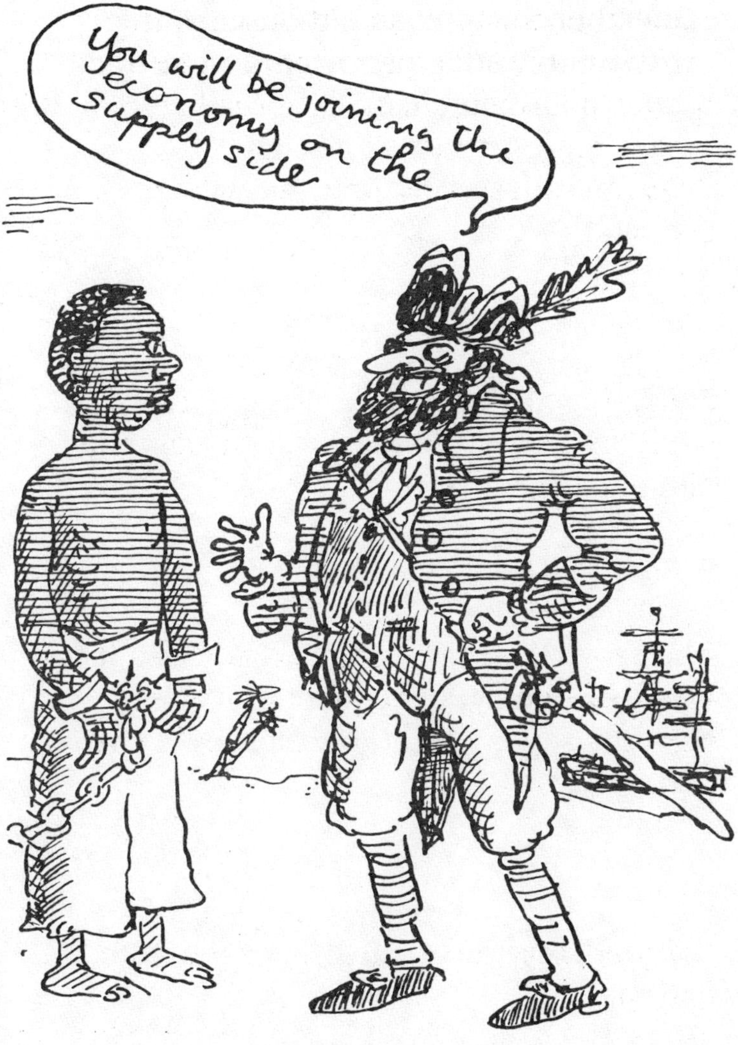
You will be joining the economy on the supply side

Beethoven: an example of what, without any state nannying, can be achieved by the deaf.

VII

Undesirable elements

Boston Tea Party: frustrated at their chronic inability to make a decent cup of tea, crazed colonists threw chests of the stuff into Boston harbour.

The Boston Tea Party: this was made possible by a grocer's shop.

Boston Tea Party: a fund-raising event for Lincolnshire Conservatives.

History confirms that we always encouraged our colonies to move to independence. Why, in the case of our American cousins we even provided a magnificent tea-party to start the whole movement off.

George Washington's great weakness was his inability to be economical with the truth.

Marie Antoinette's famous words reveal not only a concern for the diet of the ordinary Parisian in the street, but also a recognition of the need for *choice*.

She wouldn't have allowed them to eat
cake if they hadn't had a good square
meal beforehand.

Of course, the **French revolution** would
never have happened if they'd had capital
punishment.

The **guillotine:** a quick and humane
form of capital punishment directed at
the wrong class of people in the late 18th
century.

To this day, many, many French people
come up to me and say "Thank you, Mrs
Thatcher and thank you Britain" for Sir
Percy Blakeney who saved so many of
their antecedents from the vile Mister
Guillotin and his bloodthirsty followers.

Roberts hath a fcheme to break up the machines ufing only market forces!

When **Haiti** was run by France — of course, this was before the French Revolution — it was a very, very prosperous place. Then they got independence and they've been paying for it ever since. You had the Duvaliers, and they were bad enough, goodness knows, but at least you had stability. Now nobody knows what's going on.

When **Napoleon Bonaparte** referred to the British as a nation of shopkeepers he was paying tribute to those entrepreneurial skills which have helped to make our economy what it is today (and eventually produced some of the finest politicians in the land).

The odious Corsican Tyrant had to be stopped, otherwise he would have built the Channel Tunnel with public money.

The **Little Big Horn:** loony left ecology party red activists massacre thin blue line serving eviction notice.

The **Combination Laws** were introduced by Pitt to encourage the working classes to change their underwear more often.

VIII

Our gallant lads

When **Nelson** put the telescope to his blind eye to spurn the advice of the moaning minnies, he provided an inspiring example of gut conviction to leaders in later generations.

Battle of Copenhagen: a triumph over the massed naval might of a war-mongering power bent on world domination (the Danes), posing an immediate threat to Our Boys. Rejoice!

Battle of Trafalgar: a very neccessary operation regularly conducted by our gallant police officers to remove rabble-rousers and other riff-raff from the foot of that tall monument to some little man.

The Duke of Wellington: originator of the Thatcherite belief that the best way to deal with people across the Channel is to put the boot in.

Battle of Waterloo: entirely the responsibility of the railway unions.

Before you boast about **Napoleon,** just remember that Idi Amin was Sandhurst-trained.

1812: a British military expedition visited Washington, demonstrating the full warmth of the special relationship with the United States.

The **War of Jenkins' Ear:** a squalid little episode in Alliance politics.

Boer War? Don't know why we fought it. After all, they're on *our* side.

IX

Victorian values

Britain reached its zenith in the early 19th century when there were 200 capital offences. Babylon had capital punishment, too. Witness the hanging gardens.

Highland landlords in the early 19th century were the first to show concern about animal welfare.

Sending small children down the mines

and into factories engendered respect for authority and a sense of responsibility.

Picking oakum was money for old rope.

The purpose-built workhouses provided by the **Poor Laws** were home-from-home for the happy residents.

The Victorians showed their concern for improving physical exercise in young boys by encouraging them to climb chimneys.

The employment of child chimney sweeps led to the eventual British conquest of Everest.

The **truck system** of paying workers
with vouchers that could only be spent
in shops owned by their employers was
devised by philanthropic industrialists in
order to protect their workers from
diseases caused by over-indulgence in
rich foods.

1814: **George Stephenson** constructed
his first locomotive. Utterly insignificant.

George Stephenson: unsuccesful
inventor; failed to come up with the idea
of the motor car.

Those six fine gentlemen from the
obscure Dorset village of **Tolpuddle**
contributed so much to the development
of agricultural organisation that they

received a Royal Commission to practise
their skills in one of Britain's major
colonies.

In 1834 the Government was so
concerned about the condition of
agricultural labourers in Dorset that they
sent six men from Tolpuddle on a long
holiday to Australia, passage paid.

Australians speak English today
because the British workforce of the
18th century was skilled, mobile and
highly-motivated.

The alleged transportation to the
colonies of a certain class of person was
merely the voluntary relocation of
workers from areas of high

unemployment, thus reviving the
economy.

1824: repeal of all laws restricting
combinations of workmen. The sole
advantage gained by this measure was
the subsequent development of more
healthy forms of underwear.

Opium Wars: in 1839 the Chinese tried
unsuccessfully to prevent Britain
importing pain-killing drugs into China.

During the Opium Wars our great nation
stood full-square behind free trade,
helping to nurture what has become one
of today's international success stories.

The Chinese people wanted opium and we fought for their right to have it. In gratitude they gave us Hong Kong.

The Opium Wars were yet another example of Britain promoting freedom of choice for Chinese individuals.

Social historians agree that the experimental introduction of *cuisine minceur* into **Ireland** in the 1840s, with the aim of raising the level of nutritional sophistication, lacked adequate presentational expertise, and was probably an idea whose time had not yet come.

Between 1845 and 1848, so concerned was the British government about the harmful effects of high-fat foods such as bacon and dairy produce upon the health of Irish peasants that, potato blight notwithstanding, these and other risky home-produced foods were exported conscientiously as usual.

The **Gold Rush:** a splendid opportunity for small investors, some of whom were, unfortunately, eaten by bears. An inspiration for my own administration.

The **Red Indians** had reservations — but who wouldn't with so many white trespassers on their land?

During the Boer War the British government provided free holiday camp-type accommodation for thousands of civilians.

Balfour, the Conservative leader, lost three successive elections. Men!

Red Flag Act: almost brought traffic to a complete standstill; very much an indictment of Labour's transport policies.

Land Enclosure Acts: the first signs of a Green policy.

Plimsoll Line: another misguided example of levelling down at the expense of free competition.

The **Charge of the Light Brigade** was about £250 each - without exemptions for disability.

The assassination of **Abraham Lincoln** shows the sheer waste of supporting the arts in any way.

After all, **Eiffel** based his tower on Mr Blackpool's.

By sending children up chimneys the Victorians encouraged the young to rise by their own efforts.

Peterloo, 1819: an early example of voluntary euthanasia by 11 peasants.

We do so admire the courageous action of the emergency services at Peterloo.

The workhouse was a really good
example of a Youth Training Scheme
(YTS). People were taught the skills
necessary to work in the market place
and not to ask for more unless they had
earned it.

The workhouse: a form of sheltered
housing for the indigent; the zenith of
Victorian social philanthropy.

Public schools: the brilliant scheme
hatched in the mid-19th century by
those establishment figures who
preached that "the family" was the
epicentre and mainstay of civilised life.

Wilberforce's campaign against slavery:
a sorry example of how the moaning

minnies and leftwing idealists can disrupt free market forces and frustrate the entrepreneurs who make Britain great.

X

The Age of Enlightenment

The **Russian Revolution** resulted from a failure not of policies but of presentation.

World War I: failed to live up to expectations. It neither ended other wars; nor ended by Christmas, 1914. And it cost more than anyone had budgeted for it.

The Somme: yet another example of British-led European initiative becoming bogged down in what passes for a French agricultural system.

Britain and Germany spent millions on huge battle fleets but only got one decent battle out of them. This was a poor return on the money; perhaps Admirals Jellicoe and Scheer should have been paid by results.

If the trains had been nationalised in 1917 **Lenin** would never have reached Petrograd in time.

East-West relations would be very different if **Trotsky** had not committed suicide.

The **Wall Street Crash:** just another blip.

The civil rights record of **Joseph Stalin** wasn't all that bad. We all have to deal with wets.

The **Jallianwala Bagh Massacre:** This is what happens when soldiers set their sights too low.

Alexander Fleming accidentally discovered penicillin whilst unsuccessfully attempting to invent Mr Whippy ice cream.

Marie Curie's failure to find a military

use for radioactivity did, however, benefit
the NHS.

Dunkirk: a triumph, brought about by
the arming of the British and the legging
of the French.

Dunkirk: another triumph for
deregulated shipping.

Never has so much been owed by so
many to so few: a policy for the Big Five.

The **Battle of Brittan:** in the end, Leon
didn't put up much of a fight.

Very stupidly, the Russians put all their money on HMS Edinburgh, which sank. They therefore became too poor to stop the German invasion and were unable to do much to help win the war.

The **Fall of Singapore:** It didn't. It was pushed.

Pearl Harbour: following the recommendation of their budget advisors, the US Navy employed cheap oriental labour to decommission surplus naval stock.

Just look what happened the last time we had a single European market and common currency — we had to go over in 1944 and sort them out.

How best could a patriotic girl work for an Allied victory in World War II? By going up to Oxford and getting her degree, of course.

Mussolini's obsession with the efficiency of the train service was his downfall. I shall not make the same mistake.

One must not forget that the explosions at **Hiroshima** and Nagasaki gave the Japanese a tremendous lead in urban renewal.

The partitioning of **India** and Pakistan was a prime example of the creation of genuine competition from the privatisation of a state-owned monopoly.

Labour **health legislation** made many
people wear disfiguring spectacles,
hearing aids and false teeth. These
burdens were removed from the poor by
the Tories in the 1980s.

The NHS: an attenuated health service
should make Britain one of the healthiest
nations, due to natural selection.

**House Un-American Affairs
Committee:** a brilliant scheme to
establish a right-thinking consensus,
subverted by wishy-washy liberals who
put personalities before principles.

J. Edgar Hoover, during almost 50
years of devoted service to his great
nation, demonstrated beyond any shadow

THIS IS ALL A SIDE-EFFECT OF NATIONAL PROSPERITY

of doubt that no right-thinking person
person has to fear being wire-tapped or
blackmailed by any government
dedicated to the principles of individual
initiative and democracy.

Suez: a magnificent campaign, with only
one serious casualty. This was, quite
unaccountably, the prime minister.
Impossible to understand.

Harold Macmillan was a most
unbusinesslike prime minister. He gave
away large pieces of the British Empire,
instead of breaking it up into manageable
chunks and selling it back to the natives.

Remember, it was **Marks & Spencer**
sparkling wines that inspired the French
to produce champagne.

The Americans went to **Vietnam** as liberators but the natives were hostile and treacherous and when fired upon did not scruple to retaliate.

The Vietcong: natives of south-east Asia who resorted to actual killing of Americans sent with a mission to improve the lot of their deprived people.

Had private industry rather than government been responsible for arts funding, China's **Cultural Revolution** would not have happened.

1968: students demonstrated eagerly in support of a system of government loans.

Richard Nixon: an upright and moral man of the highest integrity, tragically destroyed by an unfounded and malicious smear campaign.

Abolition of free **school milk** in 1973: a health improvement measure designed to reduce cholesterol levels in children.

The **Falklands Campaign:** led to a glorious victory. The armed forces came out of it well, too.

The **Belgrano** posed a direct threat to the Task Force.

General election, 1983: a triumph for

the social and economic policies of the Conservative Party.

Irish Football League: Guildford 4, Birmingham 6 (after injury time).

Westland letter leak: an innocent misunderstanding between civil servants which unfortunately embroiled senior members of the Government.

I would think some great industrialists of the past would agree when I say that history is bunk.

Contributors

John Aldridge, Ken Alexander, Henry Aughton, Jim Badman, Michael Ball, Mike Baker, Patricia Baker, Michael Ball, Basil Banks, Alan Beattie, Christopher Bell, Stephen Bell, Freddy Bennett, Andrew Berkerey, Fiona Berryman, Allan Bishop, Beata Bishop, Chas Bloomfield, Guy Bowden, Aubrey Bramson, John Brown, Freda Bunce, Lionel Burman, Paul Burns, Ian Butler, Donald Campbell, Gerard Campbell, Morag Campbell, Winifred Carpenter, Kathy Chater, Bernard Clark, L. Clarke, J. N. Connor, Janet Cowan, J. H. Curley, Eddie Curran, P. T. Daniels, Mrs G. Dawson, Fred Diaz, Joan Donaldson, Andy Donkersley, Alan Dougherty, I. Ducasse, William Duffy, Paul Edwards, Mona Edwards, Michael Elcock, C Ellenby, Malcolm Elliott, Malcolm Elliott, R. J. Ellis, Linda Fettes, D. Fisher, B. H. Fookes, Imogen Forster,

Chris du Feu, Brenda Game, J. Gannon, Tim Goodwin,
Tim Gotsell, James Grainger, J. Green, Derek Gregory,
O. Grender, Olive Hall, Jeremy Hawthorn, Sheila
Haywood, Avril Hesson, David Hitchin, T. E. Hobday,
John and Elaine Hopkinson, David Hughes, D. Hughes,
E. Hughes, Frederick Hughes, Jean Humphries, Phil
Hutchinson, Lee Inman, S. Jacobs, John Jenkinson,
Frank Johnson, Richard Joynson, Rashid Karapiet, Gary
Kentish, David Kerr, John King, R. A. King, S. Knight,
Harpreet Kohli, Graham Larkbey, Nigel Lee, Jo
Letchford, Elspeth Loades, Fred Lowe, Julia Luff, Ian
Lygo, John W. Lyle, N. Mackenzie, Hubert Marsden,
Deirdre Mason, Jane Matthews, Ann McBride, Tim
McCullen, Iain McLean, Eileen McNally, Bernadette
Meaden, Stella Miles, Edgar Miller, M. Miller, C. Lloyd
Mills, Peter Milner, David Minch, Mike Mitchell, Ged
Moran, G. Morris, Mike Myers, Steve Nesbitt, Bernard
Newgrosh, Paul A. Newman, J. A. Newton, Joseph
Nicholas, B. O'Brien, Joyce Parr, Mary Pascoe, Lindsay
Pearce, Stewart Philbrock, Colin Pilkington, Lawrence
Platt, Matt Plesch, Brian Poag, Peter Porteous, Rod
Prince, Christopher Prior, David Pugh, Ty Raeburn,
Mary Raftery, Morys Raine, H. Rapp, N. Ratcliffe,
William Reimbold, Gary Reynolds, Stephen Rochester,
Eric and Esther Roome, Mary Routh, Sheila Routley,
Alan Rowe, Betty Rubinstein, Mary Sanderson, Jessica
Saraga, Colin Savage, A. Scriven, Grace Shelley, G.
Shepherd, Ted Sheppard, John Sheeran, Paul Sheridan,
Jill Shields, Peter and Audrey Sillis, Ian Simmons, Brian

Smith, J. Smith, Michael J. Smith, Steve Sneyd, Margaret
Squires, Frank Stainthorp, A. Steal, John Sweeney,
Sophie Swingewood, Doris Taylor, Peter Tetley, M. H.
Thatcher, Arwyn Thomas, Barbara Thompson, Thomas
Thompson, Lee Turley, Norman Tyrell, Sandra Wallace,
David Graham Walker, Jerry Walsh, Don Weedon, Keith
Wells, Gill Whitfield, Elizabeth Whittome, Mike Wills,
M. Wilshaw, Roger Woddis, Arthur Wong, Maureen
Wood, Malcolm Wren, Mark Yates, Ivor Yeloff,
Grenville Young, Peter Young.